Progressive Debate

BILAL QURESHI

ACTIVE

1

도서출판 청람

Preface

The Progressive Debate series consists of a string of articles on a variety of daily life issues in order to offer two-sided perspectives in each unit which can help learners connect their background knowledge to the topic. The most distinguished feature of this book series is the combination of warm up, pre reading and listening, and main comprehension exercises which develop learners' fluency and accuracy. These comprehension exercises allow students to fully grasp the topic in depth through the course of the whole series. The step by step progression of comprehension exercises engages learners to develop their knowledge for a more evocative conversation. These exercises lead students to develop their own unique perspectives about the topics and engage in meaningful conversation as a final goal.

Reading

A variety of daily life topics with lots of interesting and eye catching vocabulary words are one of the best features of this series of books. All articles are followed by a series of exercises that will certainly help learners improve their comprehension skills.

Discussion

Progressive Debate has been specifically designed to target discussion based classes. It further emphasizes students' need for all four components of language including speaking, reading, writing, and listening.

Writing

Through a systematic organization of comprehension exercises, learners are able to produce a well-organized paragraph in written form.

Step-by-step execution plan for Progressive Debate in Classroom

1. Brainstorm about the topic using questions given in the warm-up section.
2. Get ready for reading by completing pre-reading exercises. Match the target words to their synonyms and explore the meaning of useful expressions given in the contents.
3. Read or listen the content and find the main idea.
4. Find the answers to the comprehension questions in each article.
5. Fill in the blanks using the given words.
6. Complete the sentences by matching one from each section in exercise 3.
7. Fill in the blanks and complete the summary of the article. After filling in the blanks, summarize the important points of the whole article orally.
8. Find grammatical errors in sentences and correct them.
9. Engage your group mates in a discussion using the questions given in exercise 6. These questions will help learners develop their own opinions about the topics. Try to ask more follow up questions to explore your peers' opinions.
10. Read the question in exercise 7 carefully and brainstorm for ideas with your peers. Complete the writing task as a homework assignment.

Components

Student book & Online Audio Recordings for each Article.

Key Feature

The Progressive Debate Active series is a three level, speaking oriented series of books for intermediate proficiency level English learners.These books include a series of interesting and relevant daily life topics to help English learners enhance their communication skills by participating in classroom debate. The articles contain a wide range of vocabulary, useful expressions, and step-by-step comprehension exercises to help learners develop their opinions and express their ideas in more logical and fun ways. This book series proves to be the best solution for English learners' fluency development because of its unique organization of exercises that help to develop learners' ability and knowledge gradually.

Progressive Debate

Table of Content

Unit 01 Is Eating Peeled Fruit Healthy? 1
Unit 02 Should Coins Disappear? 8
Unit 03 Should Fast Food Be Banned? 15
Unit 04 Do Tests Help Students? 22
Unit 05 Should Malls Ban Teenage Shoppers? 29
Unit 06 Is Illegal Downloading a Problem? 36
Unit 07 Do Children Need a Smartphone Curfew? 43
Unit 08 Can Punishment Deter Adolescent Crimes? 50
Unit 09 Does Deforestation Help Humanity? 57
Unit 10 Is Online Banking Helpful? 64
Unit 11 Can Korea be More Multicultural? 71
Unit 12 Is Eating Out Better Than Eating In? 78
Unit 13 Are Driverless Buses Reliable? 85
Unit 14 Do We Need Free Wi-Fi? 92
Unit 15 Is Drinking a Problem in Korea? 99
Unit 16 Are Solar Panels Effective? 106

Unit 01 Is Eating Peeled Fruit Healthy?

Warm Up Exercises

01 Answer these questions.

1. Name at least 3 fruits that you like.
2. Name at least 3 kinds of nutrients.
3. What are pesticides?

02 Put the foods in right column.

Tomato, Spinach, Apple, Cabbage, Onion, Persimmon, Grape, Passion fruit, Cucumber

Fruits	Vegetables

Pre-Vocabulary Exercises

1 Match the words to their similar meaning.

1. Calories	a. to take away
2. Deprive	b. advantageous or good
3. Stomach	c. amount of energy food has
4. Nutrition	d. the skin
5. Peel (n)	e. the condition of the body
6. Health	f. belly
7. Benefit	g. food and nourishment

2 Find the meaning of the following phrases.

1. Health benefits ____________________
2. In order to ____________________
3. Unpeeled fruits ____________________
4. Good percentage ____________________

Is Eating Peeled Fruit Healthy?

There is a long standing myth that there are some fruits which require more calories to digest than they actually supply to our body. Unfortunately, that is totally untrue. Fruit, with or without peels, is one of the major components and probably the most reliable sources of nutrition in our food cycle. Peeling fruit has been a controversial issue among fruit lovers for a long time. Some believe peeled fruits are healthy and better tasting whereas others claim that peeling fruit means missing out on lots of nutrition that a fruit contains in the peel. How do you eat your fruit?

People who believe that peeled fruit possesses more health benefits claim that the skin of some fruits is too thick for our stomach to digest. They believe that the skin of fruits like apples, persimmons, and mangoes is too hard and causes excess labor for our stomachs in order to digest them. In addition, the amount of nutrients found in these fruits' skin is very low. Second, a lot of pesticides are sprayed on the fruit in order to keep bugs and other harmful insects away from damaging them. Some of these pesticides stay on the fruit skin even though people mostly wash them before eating. Therefore, they claim peeled fruits are healthier than unpeeled fruits.

Opponents claim that peeling above mentioned fruits may deprive them from their actual health benefits. First, a good percentage of nutrition is stored in the skin. That means that when we peel them, we are throwing away a lot of nutrition. The skin also contains fiber which is crucial for our bodies' health. Second, some fruit peels are tremendously helpful for the natural treatment of diseases. For example, apple peels contain antioxidants that prevents cancer. Most fruits' skins are a rich source of minerals and vitamins with numerous health benefits.

Following the discussion above, it can be concluded that washing fruit with water carefully cleans all sorts of chemicals that are sprayed on fruits. The peel of the fruits is considered a good source of vitamin, minerals, and antioxidants. However, people with sensitive health conditions may prefer to peel the fruit before consuming.

Main Exercises

1 Answer the questions.

Q1. Is it true that some fruits take more calories to digest than they actually supply to the body?

Q2. Why do people spray pesticide on fruit?

Q3. What kind of nutrients does the fruit skin contain?

Q4. What diseases can antioxidants in apple peels prevent?

Q5. What are the benefits of washing fruits with water carefully?

2 Fill up the blanks using the words below.

calories *peel* *health* *benefits* *stomach*

1. Matt slipped on a banana ....
2. His .... hurt because he had too much soda.
3. Eating too much fast food can cause serious .... problems.
4. The .... of travelling by bus is that you can save money.
5. French fries are high on .... and low on nutrients.

3 Match the phrases to those given below.

1. A vegan diet has health benefits.
2. We should recycle garbage in order to.
3. A good percentage of people believe.
4. Eating unpeeled fruit.

a. Takes some time to adapt to.

b. That aliens do not exist.

c. Because it makes us eat less fat and more vitamins.

d. Protect the environment.

4 Summary

Fill the blanks up using the words given below and complete the summary.

nutrients, stomachs, cancer, source, chemicals, skin, completely

Fruit, peeled or unpeeled, is one of the most important part in our diet. Some people claim that the ________ of some fruits cause a lot of work for our ________ to digest them. They also say that a lot of pesticide is sprayed onto the fruit and they do not get ________washed off. However, other people believe that it is better to eat fruit unpeeled, as most of the ________ are stored in the skin. Not only that, the skin of some fruits, such as apples are extremely helpful in treating diseases like________. Although opinions may differ between people, it can be known that washing fruits carefully with water can get rid of most of the ________ on the fruit, and that the peel of the fruit is considered as a good ________ of vitamins and other good nutrients.

5 Find the mistake in each sentence and correct the underlined words.

1. Washing fruit with water can <u>removing</u> most of the pesticide.
2. It is untrue that some fruits <u>requiring</u> more calories to digest than they give off.
3. A lot of nutrients are <u>store</u> in the skin of the fruit.
4. Pesticide and other chemicals are <u>spray</u> on fruit to keep away insects and bugs.

6 Discussion Questions

1. Why do people eat peeled fruit?
2. Why do people eat unpeeled fruit?
3. What health benefits can we have if we only eat fruit?
4. How can eating fruit be cheaper than regular meals?
5. Are pesticides good or harmful for our health?

7 Writing Time

Is eating peeled fruits healthy or not? Provide reasons and examples to support your opinion.

Unit 02 Should Coins Disappear?

Warm Up Exercises

01 **Answer these questions**

1. What are coins made of?
2. Have you ever tried collecting coins?
3. How do you spend your coins?

02 **Put the words in right column.**

Coin, Dollar, Won, Check, Euro, Bills, Pound

Currency	Type of Money

Pre-Vocabulary Exercises

1 Match the words to their similar meaning.

1. Denomination	**a.** business between two people
2. Debit branch	**b.** branch
3. Transaction	**c.** getting rid of
4. Eliminating	**d.** to charge with a debt
5. Traditional	**e.** connections
6. Affiliations	**f.** old-style
7. Sector	**g.** classification of something

2 Find the meaning of the following phrases.

1. Paper bills ______________________________

2. Method of payment ______________________________

3. Credit card ______________________________

4. In addition ______________________________

Should Coins Disappear?

Coins were introduced as a method of payment around the 5th century BC. The invention of coins made the life much easier. Coins of different denominations are still used in almost every country. Furthermore, some countries have introduced new coins to celebrate special events in country's history. Coins also provide people feelings of connectivity to a certain culture. However, with the development of financial systems, credit cards and debit cards are used widely across the globe. This has reduced the importance of coins in the modern age. Some economists think that coins should be replaced completely with paper bills.

People who think that coins should be replaced by paper bills argue that in the modern world, coins have lost their importance. First, the production of coins is a difficult and expensive process for any government. Each government spends lots of money producing coins. Many people feel they are heavy and annoying to carry. Second, because of credit and debit cards, coins are meaningless anyway. Most people use their credit cards for shopping, eating out, traveling, etc. They do not have many chances to use cash for their purchases. In addition, most credit card companies give reward points for each transaction we make using the credit card. This tempts people even more not to use cash. Therefore, the uselessness of coins is even more evident.

On the other hand, some people insist that coins are an important part of our daily life. First, eliminating coins may cause many financial problems in the business sector. Most business deals are made in decimals and that means eliminating coins may necessitate a major change in the whole financial market structure. Second, coins are great tools to keep inflation in control. If coins are abolished, the price of items in retail market have to round up or round down. This can cause a big economic disruption in society. In addition, coins are a traditional symbol of each country that reflects country's history and cultural values.

In conclusion, besides the fact that the governments may have to bear a lot of expenses for coin production, coins are part and parcel of each society. Cultures have strong affiliations with coins. In order to maintain the traditional values, the government and the credit card companies may find better solutions to balance the use of coins and the credit cards.

Main Exercises

1 Answer the questions.

Q1. When were coins introduced as a method of payment?

Q2. What kind of benefits do credit cards offer when transactions are made?

Q3. What kind of significance does a coin reflect?

Q4. What might happen if coins are abolished in the retail market?

Q5. What kind of problems do coins have?

2 Fill up the blanks using the words below.

transaction *debit* *traditional* *eliminating* *denominations*

1. You should be careful when making a financial ………………… .
2. Some coins have high …………………. and cultural value.
3. …………………… coins altogether may yield some serious problems.
4. The 500 dollars was paid in small ………………….. .
5. Credit cards or ……………… cards are common because they are easy to carry.

3 Match the phrases to those given below.

1. In addition to not making rash buying decisions,
2. He decided to use his visa card as a method of payment.
3. Credit card may be a convenient way for paying for stuff.
4. Paper bills are more commonly used in shops.

a. Saving spare coins can be a good way to spend money.

b. However, coins are often used in vending machines.

c. Because he did not have any cash on him.

d. But card fees can become pretty frightening.

4 Summary

Fill the blanks up using the words given below and complete the summary.

meaningless, importance, financial, traditional, producing, expensive

Coins were introduced in the fifth century, and it made life much easier. However, with the development of ________ systems and credit cards, it has reduced the ________ of coins in the modern age. Some people think that coins should be replaced because it is ________to make, and they are__________. The opposition claims that they are a part of daily life, and will cause financial problems. Also, coins are a __________ symbol of each country as well. Although the government may have to pay a lot for ________ coins, the government and the credit card company must find a better solution to balance the use of coins and credit cards.

5 Find the mistake in each sentence and correct the underlined words.

1. Producing of coins are a difficult and expensive process.
2. Eliminating coins may cause finance problems in the business sector.
3. Sometimes special coins are made to celebration certain events.
4. It is a good idea to storing spare change in jars.

6 Discussion Questions

Q1. Do you think relying solely on credit cards is a good idea? Why or why not?

Q2. What might we do with existing coins if coins are replaced?

Q3. What are the disadvantages of using paper bills?

Q4. What are some good ways to deal with spare change?

7 Writing Time

Is it a good idea to eliminate coins? Will it make life easier for us to buy the things we want, or will it leave in a bigger trouble? What are the pros and cons of using coins? Provide reasons and examples to support your opinion.

Unit 03 Should Fast Food Be Banned?

Warm Up Exercises

01 Answer these questions.

1. What is a fast food?
2. Name at least 3 most common fast foods.
3. Name at least 3 fast food restaurants that you know.

02 Put the foods in right column.

Fried chicken, Spaghetti, Curry, Sushi, Coke, Ice cream, Pizza, Hamburger

Fast Food	Slow Food

Pre-Vocabulary Exercises

1 Match the words to their similar meaning.

1. Consumption	a. eating habits
2. Opportunity	b. recognition
3. Moderation	c. prohibit
4. Dietary habits	d. the using up of a resource
5. Considerable	e. chance
6. Ban	f. the avoidance of access
7. Identity	g. significant

2 Find the meaning of the following phrases.

1. Rapid growth ______________________________
2. Leads toward ______________________________
3. Harmful effects ______________________________
4. Boosting economy ______________________________

Should Fast Food Be Banned?

Food that can be prepared quickly and easily is called fast food. Fast foods are quick alternatives to home-made meals. Fast food has gained a lot of popularity over the past three decades. In the United States, fast food makes up a considerable part of people's diet. Common fast food choices include pizza, burgers, fried potatoes, and soft drinks. In this age of rapid advancement when people are so busy, fast food has become an important part of meals and snacks. However, there are varying opinions on fast food consumption regarding its benefits and harmful effects.

Proponents of fast food argue that it is a growing trend because of its increasing popularity among young people and the widespread business opportunities related to the fast food industry. First, most fast food restaurants serve food within 5 minutes of placing an order and that saves time for busy people. In addition, fast food is mostly tasty with an attractive smell. Fast food restaurants are located at busy spots in many countries. These stores are easily accessible to people and most of these stores are open from early morning till late at night. Second, fast food is becoming an ideal business venture that helps to boost economy. Many people are engaged in this business and it is a good workplace for students who look for part-time jobs.

Other people argue that fast food consumption should be reduced for many health and social reasons. First, fast food causes lots of health problems. People who regularly consume fast food face illnesses including diabetes, asthma, and heart problems. Fast food contains lots of calories that lead to obesity. Obesity is becoming a major health concern in advanced countries where fast food industries are growing rapidly. Second, fast food may detract from the traditional food culture.

Each country has its own traditional foods that are considered part of national identity. The growing fast food industry is a big concern for local and traditional foods industries in many countries.

In conclusion, fast food is a growing trend that is becoming popular among people of all ages. However, maintaining a balance between fast food and regular food is important. Following the concerns that are related to fast food consumption, moderation is important for maintaining a healthy society.

Main Exercises

1 Answer the questions.

Q1. When did fast food gain popularity?

Q2. How quickly are most fast foods served?

Q3. How can fast food restaurants be helpful for students?

Q4. Which diseases can too much fast food consumption cause?

Q5. How can fast food harm a country?

2 Fill up the blanks using the words below.

consume *opportunity* *moderation* *ban* *identity*

1. My sister ……………….…. too much time for taking a shower.

2. Hanbok is a cultural ………..……………. of Korea.

3. He eats in ……………………. to stay healthy.

4. The government decided to …………………. smoking nearby schools.

5. She considered it a great ……………… to interview her university professor.

3 Match the phrases to those given below.

1. It can hurt cultural identity.

2. A regular consumption of fast food can cause health problem.

3. Fast food are good alternatives of home food.

4. Fast food is an ideal business.

a. Because home food takes too long to cook.

b. It is growing very fast.

c. Because less and less people eat traditional food.

d. Obesity is becoming a major problem in advanced countries.

4 Summary

Fill the blanks up using the words given below and complete the summary.

replacement, taste, economic, obesity, related to, minutes, restaurants, banned, balance

Fast foods are quick ______________ of home-made meals that take a long time to prepare. Some people believe fast foods are great meal options for busy people. Most fast foods are served in 5 ______________ after placing the order. Easy access and variety of ______________ options offered by fast food ______________ make it attractive for most young people. Furthermore, fast food businesses are providing great ______________ opportunities for many people. Whereas, the opponents of fast food argue that fast food should be ______________ because of negative effects on health and society. Fast food is the biggest reason of ___________ that triggers illnesses like diabetes, heart disease, and asthma. In addition, fast food culture hurts country's traditional food culture and businesses _____________ it. In short, fast food is becoming a part of our daily life. Therefore, keeping a ____________ between our fast food consumption and regular food to stay healthy is important.

5 Find the mistake in each sentence and correct it by reshaping the underlined words.

1. Fast food is become a popular trend in many countries.
2. People who regular consume fast food face illnesses.
3. Fast food business is provide economic opportunities to many people.
4. Most fast foods are serve in 5 minutes after placing order.
5. Most fast food restaurants are locate in busy areas.

6 Discussion Questions

1. Do you think fast food will take over slow food?
2. How can we enjoy fast food and still stay healthy?
3. Why is fast food more attractive than some of slow foods?
4. How is fast food related to obesity? Why is obesity a problem?
5. What are the health benefits of slow foods?

7 Writing Time

Why is fast food culture spreading at a rapid pace? Is it a healthy development or a harmful trend? What are pros and cons of fast food culture? Provide reasons and examples to support your opinion.

Unit 04 Do Tests Help Students?

Warm Up Exercises

01 **Answer these questions.**

1. What is a test?
2. Do you like tests? Why or why not?
3. Name at least 3 kinds of tests.

02 **Put the words in right column.**

Quiz, Exam, English, History, Midterms, P.E., Math

Tests	Subjects

Pre-Vocabulary Exercises

1 Match the words to their similar meaning.

1. Analyze	**a.** capability
2. Learner	**b.** attempt
3. Aptitude	**c.** working together
4. Collaboration	**d.** assignment
5. Projects	**e.** initiate
6. Effort	**f.** student
7. Trigger	**g.** gadget
8. Tool	**h.** examine

2 Find the meaning of the following phrases.

1. Unneeded competition ____________________

2. Unfair judgement ____________________

3. Positive attitude ____________________

4. Based on ____________________

Do Tests Help Students?

Testing is one of the most common ways of assessing learners' progress all over the world. Test scores determine learner's'performance during a certain time of study. However, some people think that testing is an unreasonable measure to judge someone's aptitude. They claim that assessing learners through some educational projects boosts their creativity and it is a more practical way of learning. Will the day come when there are no tests, only projects?

Opponents of testing systems consider tests an unfair judgment tool for students'progress. First, tests create a divide and promote feelings of unneeded competition. Students try to get higher scores than their counterparts without understanding what they are studying. Tests require memorization skills that damage creativity in students. Therefore, assigning learners projects to complete within a specific time seems like a great way to examine their progress. Second, assessment through projects helps learners to collaborate rather than compete against each other. Collaboration triggers a positive attitude towards learning and understanding. It teaches learners teamwork and responsibility.

People who view tests as the only way to analyze learners' progress present two reasons why. First, they think that testing students is a very subjective way to evaluate learners'effort during a course. Tests distinguish those who work hard and invest their energy in studying from those who do not pay much attention to studying and spend most of their time playing. In addition, testing students is also a great way for teacher to measure students'performance and score them accordingly. Second, tests are a great drive for students to study hard with determination. Tests create competition which helps learners to invest more effort into their learning.

Furthermore, tests initiate willingness among lazy students who do not want to work hard during the term time.

In conclusion, assessment in education is mostly based on testing students. However, projects could be a great way to assess learners'progress if implemented carefully. Governments and the educators should find better alternatives that cause less stress and trigger more creativity in students.

Main Exercises

1 Answer the questions.

Q1. What is the most common way to assess a learner's progress?

Q2. What negative effect does memorization skills have on students?

Q3. Why assessing learners through educational projects is a better way than tests?

Q4. How does a test encourage students to study hard?

Q5. Is it possible to distinguish those who work hard from those who do not through tests?

2 Fill up the blanks using the words below.

learner *aptitude* *projects* *trigger* *tool*

1. She is a fast ...., she memorizes everything quickly.
2. Memorization is a great learning..................... when studying for a test.
3. My school uses group .... to assess students.
4. Some students show great .... in memorizing.
5. A reward is the best way to .... enthusiasm amongst students.

3 Match the phrases to those given below.

1. Keeping a positive attitude at all times
2. Unfair judgement often occurs
3. Based on these researches
4. If unneeded competition occurs

a. It may result in dire consequences.

b. Will guarantee success.

c. It can be known that tests may not be the best way to judge students.

d. When a person has prejudice against somebody else.

4 Summary

Fill the blanks up using the words given below and complete the summary.

unnecessary, assessing, solution, responsibility, distinguish, initiate, collaborate, competition, creativity

Testing is one of the most common ways of _________ one's progress, which is used all over the world. However, some people say that it is an unreasonable method to judge someone's aptitude and that educational projects are a better __________, because it creates a divide and promote ___________ competition. Not only that, assessment through projects help students learn to __________ with each other, as well as teamwork and___________. Advocates of tests claim that tests have the power to _________ those who work hard and put effort into studying from those who do not. Also, it serves as a great drive for students by creating __________ which helps learners invest more time into learning, and __________ willingness for lazy students. Currently, assessment is mostly based on tests, but projects may be a good solution as well. The government and educators should find better solution which gives less stress and triggers more ________ amongst students.

5 Find the mistake in each sentence and correct the underlined words.

1. Tests creating competition which helps learners to invest more efforts into learning
2. Collaboration triggers a positive attitude towards learn and understanding.
3. Assessment in education is most based on testing students.
4. Students need a good understood of the material.
5. Schools should find ways to trigger creative in students.

6 Discussion Questions

1. Do you think group projects are a better way to assess students than tests? Why or why not?
2. How can we study efficiently for tests?
3. Why does unnecessary competition occur? How can it be reduced?
4. Does a high test score necessarily mean that a person is a hard worker?
5. What kind of projects can be assigned to English language students?

7 Writing Time

Are school projects a good way to evaluate students' learning? What are the pros and cons of school projects for evaluation? State reasons and provide examples to support your opinion.

Unit 05 Should Malls Ban Teenage Shoppers?

Warm Up Exercises

01 **Answer these questions.**

1. What is a shopping mall?
2. Name at least 3 shopping malls that you know.
3. Name at least 3 sections in a shopping mall.

02 **Put the words in right column.**

Dried persimmon, Coat, Jacket, Suit, Rice cake, Mackerel, Tie

Food	Clothing

Pre-Vocabulary Exercises

1 Match the words to their similar meaning.

1. atmosphere	a. false impression
2. influx	b. unfairness
3. discomfort	c. feeling uneasy
4. customer	d. consumer
5. maintain	e. keep
6. prejudice	f. mood
7. discrimination	g. flowing in

2 Find the meaning of the following phrases.

1. Self-esteem ____________________
2. Human rights ____________________
3. Rush hour ____________________
4. Pleasant time ____________________

Should Malls Ban Teenage Shoppers?

Shopping malls are generally considered to be a great place to shop and have pleasant time with family or friends. Especially, on weekends, malls are overcrowded with shoppers of all ages. Malls provide a nice shopping atmosphere to not only shoppers but also prove to be a great place for young teenagers to hang out with their friends. Sometimes the influx of teenagers during rush hour causes problems for mall administration. Should teenagers without parents be allowed to go to malls?

Some people think that children should be banned from entering big malls. First, the ban will help maintain security in the mall. Sometimes teens steal or damage stuff in the mall. Putting a ban on teenagers entering the mall may help addressing these issues. Second, the ban will also help control those teenagers who fight in malls. The fights that happen in malls sometimes attract police attention, which causes discomfort not only for the businesses but also for the shoppers who go there to shop or enjoy a meal with family.

Opponents of banning teenagers from entering malls argue that the ban is unfair and deprives children of their human rights. First, some teenagers go to the mall for shopping. They might be buying presents for their parent's birthday or shopping for Christmas present for their friends. Banning them will keep them from their customers'right to shop. Second, banning teenagers from entering malls without parents will give them feelings of discrimination. Teenagers are an important part of each society and they are to become future leaders of the country. Banning them from entering malls will hurt their self-esteem.

In conclusion, teenagers are an important part of any society who need to be treated equally. Having a prejudice against them will not only hurt their self-esteem but also deprive them of their human rights. Therefore, both mall administration and teenagers should respect each other and find a solution that protects rights and security of both sides.

Main Exercises

1 Answer the questions.

Q1. What benefits do malls provide?

Q2. What negative effects do fights that happen in the mall have?

Q3. How can banning teenagers from entering malls become discrimination?

Q4. Why do some teenagers go to the mall?

Q5. What kind of problems do teenagers cause in the mall?

2 Fill up the blanks using the words below.

customer *discomfort* *atmosphere* *influx* *maintain*

1. A pleasant shopping .... leads consumers to buy more items.
2. Many shops have the slogan, "the .... is the king".
3. Seller must think of many ideas to .... the number of buyers.
4. Teenager fights can cause .... for other shoppers.
5. The .... of people during the rush hour can cause problems for the mall staff.

3 Match the phrases to those given below.

1. Sitting on the bus during rush hour.
2. Having low self-esteem.
3. It is important to respect human rights during times of war.
4. People visit the mall to have a pleasant time.

a. As well as shopping for clothes or food.

b. Even though it may be hard.

c. Can have negative effects to one's mental health.

d. Is stressful because it wastes too much time.

4 Summary

Fill the blanks up using the words given below and complete the summary.

self-esteem, shopping, human rights, administration, damage, discomfort, customers, solution

Shopping malls are a great place for __________ and spending time with friends and family. A lot of teens visit the shopping mall to hang out as well. However, some people believe that teenagers should be banned from malls because not only do they steal or ________ items at the mall, but they also cause fights, which draws police attention and causes __________ for business and other __________ as well. On the other hand, those who are positive about teens at the shopping mall say that the ban is not fair and deprives them of their__________. They also claim that it may hurt their ___________ as well. Teenagers are an important part of society, and mall ________ and teenagers should respect each other while finding a _________ which works on bothsides.

5 Find the mistake in each sentence and correct the underlined words.

1. Putting a ban on teenagers enter the mall may help addressing these issues.
2. Banning teenagers from malls may low their self-esteem.
3. Fights which happen in the mall attracting police attention.
4. The mall is extreme crowded during weekends and sale seasons.
5. Mall administration and teenagers should find a solution which can satisfaction both parties.

6 Discussion Questions

1. Do you think fights at the mall are a nuisance? Why or why not?
2. Why do teenagers steal or damage goods at malls?
3. Will teenagers with low self-esteem cause problems in the future? How?
4. How can mall workers and teenagers come up with a satisfactory solution?

7 Writing Time

Some malls restrict unaccompanied teenagers from entering? What are the pros and cons of this policy? Provide reasons and examples to support your idea.

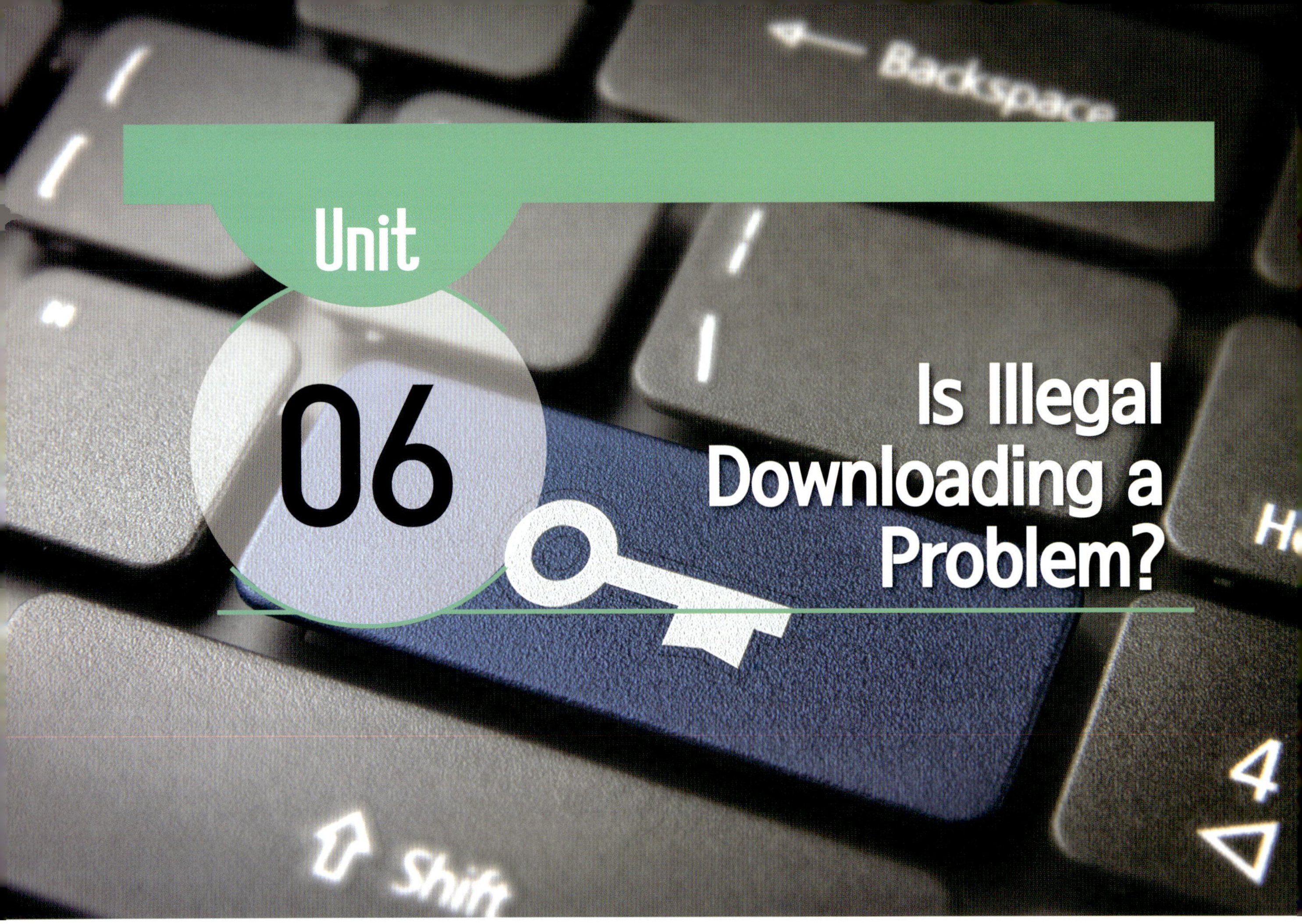

Unit 06

Is Illegal Downloading a Problem?

Warm Up Exercises

01 Answer these questions.

1. What is illegal downloading?
2. Name at least 3 kinds of media which can be downloaded through the internet.
3. Have you ever downloaded something illegally before?

02 Put the words in right column.

Music, Vase, Video, Movie, Mannequin, Artist, Games, Blanket

Downloadable	Not downloadable

Pre-Vocabulary Exercises

1 Match the words to their similar meaning.

1. Illegal
2. Downloading
3. Violate
4. Bankrupt
5. Unknown
6. Popular
7. Gateway
8. Abiding

a. following
b. to break
c. not legal
d. unidentified
e. to transfer data into a computer
f. path
g. well known
h. out of money

2 Find the meaning of the following phrases.

1. Copyright laws ______________________
2. Criminal act ______________________
3. Growing business ______________________
4. Illegal downloading ______________________

Is Illegal Downloading a Problem?

Have you ever downloaded any movie or music illegally? Illegal downloading can be viewed the same as stealing someone's stuff. Downloading movies or music illegally is becoming more and more common as internet technologies are developing rapidly. According to recent statistics, more than 50% of the music downloaded by the people age 16 to 24 is illegal. Illegal downloading is not only a growing practice by internet users but it is a growing business too. Is illegal downloading really a serious problem?

People who think illegal downloading is harmful believe that it violates copyright laws. First, it deprives the artists of their rightful income. If the artist doesn't get paid for their music, they may not have enough resources to produce artistic works again in the future. They might also go bankrupt if their sources of income are restricted. Second, illegal downloading is a criminal act that may be a gateway to other crimes in society. This can spread to other businesses eventually. In addition, each citizen is responsible to play a constructive role for nation development by abiding by the rules.

On the other hand, some people think illegal downloading has some benefits. First, unknown artists can become famous via illegal downloading. When the artistic work of new artists is downloaded and listened to by many people, they may gain popularity. This can help them to become successful. Second, illegal downloading may decrease the unevenness of access between the rich and poor in the society. If popular music is available online for free or at a very cheap price, an ordinary person may also be able to access it. This may help reducing the feelings of class distinction in society.

In conclusion, downloading music illegally is a misdeed socially and morally, but it seems like there is no way it can be stopped. The best way to solve this problem is to introduce a new framework that is acceptable for both the artists and the users. The government may regulate illegal downloading websites in order to provide benefits to both users and the artists simultaneously.

Main Exercises

1 Answer the questions.

Q1. What kind of problem occurs when an artist is not paid for his work?

Q2. What percentage of music downloads are by people aged 16 to 24?

Q3. Why do people believe that illegal downloading is harmful?

Q4. Does the writer think that illegal downloading can be stopped?

Q5. How can illegal downloading decrease the unevenness between the rich and the poor?

2 Fill up the blanks using the words below.

illegal *unknown* *abiding* *violate* *popular*

1. ………………… safety rules at the pool is important for everyone's safety and leisure.
2. The cause of the accident is still ………………….. .
3. You will go to prison if you …………………….. the law.
4. Music by idol groups are ………………….. amongst teenagers.
5. Watching movies online without paying is an ……………. method of watching movies.

3 Match the phrases to those given below.

1. Arson is a criminal act.
2. It is important to abide copyright laws.
3. The reason why people use illegal downloading.
4. The fast food industry used to be a growing business.

a. And it will be punished severely by the law.
b. And it is still growing until this day.
c. When creating any kind of creative work.
d. Is because they do not have enough money to buy the actual work itself.

4 Summary

Fill the blanks up using the words given below and complete the summary.

technology, illegal, distinction, downloading, gap, criminal, framework, abiding,

As _________ becomes more and more advanced, illegal _________ is becoming extremely common. According to statistics, over 50% of the music downloaded by people of ages between 16 to 24 is illegal. Some people believe ________ downloading is harmful because it violates copyright laws, depriving the artist of his income. Not only that, illegal downloading is a ________ act, and all citizens are responsible for helping in nation development through ________ the rules. However, others think illegal downloading could make unknown artists become well-known, and reduce the accessibility _________ between the rich and the poor, therefore reduce the feelings of class __________ in society. Illegal downloading is illegal, but it is unlikely to be stopped. Introducing a new __________which is acceptable to both users and the artist may be a good solution to this problem.

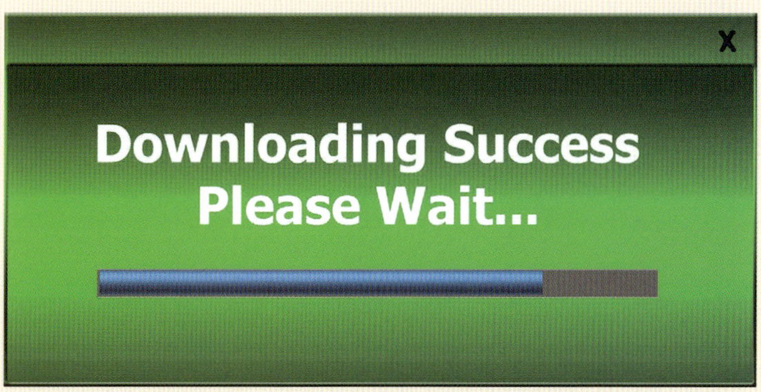

5 Find the mistake in each sentence and correct the underlined words.

1. Illegal downloading is happened a lot in today's society.
2. Uneven wealth is intensified the knowledge gap between the rich and the poor.
3. Artists produce cannot their work if they do not have enough resources.
4. Illegal downloading of music may enabling unknown artists to become famous.
5. Each citizen is responsible to play a constructive role for nation developing.

6 Discussion Questions

1. Do you think illegal downloading can be stopped? Why or why not?
2. How can we prevent illegal downloading?
3. What are some other ways unknown artists can become famous other than illegal downloading?
4. Will legalizing illegal download lessen the gap between the rich and the poor? Why or why not?
5. What are the benefits of legally downloading content?

7 Writing Time

Is downloading music illegally a serious social problem or not? Provide reasons and examples to support your answer.

Unit 07 Do Children Need a Smartphone Curfew?

Warm Up Exercises

01 **Answer these questions.**

1. What is a smartphone?
2. What does it mean by curfew?
3. Do you have a curfew?

02 **Put the words in right column.**

Bathroom, 4'o'clock, Afternoon, Café, Midnight, Half past 2, Classroom, Seaside

Time	Place

Pre-Vocabulary Exercises

1 Match the words to their similar meaning.

1. Unnecessary	**a.** a time limit
2. Curfew	**b.** forcing
3. Distraction	**c.** to cause a disturbance
4. Mitigate	**d.** to make the most of
5. Maximize	**e.** lessen
6. Browsing	**f.** searching
7. Imposing	**g.** not needed

2 Find the meaning of the following phrases.

1. Advanced countries ______________________

2. Moderate use ______________________

3. Family relationships ______________________

4. Create a balance ______________________

Do Children Need a Smartphone Curfew?

Smartphones are one of the most amazing inventions of the modern age. It is estimated that Korea has the highest rate of smartphone users among all advanced countries. Reports say that an average Korean teenager spends at least two hours every day using a smartphone. This includes using SNS applications, browsing the internet, and listening to music etc. Most experts believe that the excessive use of smartphones causes many physical and social problems for teenagers. Some experts suggest a smartphone curfew for teenagers after 9pm.

People, who think imposing a curfew on teenagers' smartphone use after 9pm could be helpful, have two main arguments. First, they think imposing a curfew may help them to focus better on their studies. Overusing smartphones may cause distractions from their studies. Some teenagers spend too much time browsing the internet and chatting with their friends. A curfew will help them to focus to complete their homework and other school activities before going to bed. Second, imposing a curfew on smartphones may help teenagers spend more time with their families. Studies on smartphone usage report that people who have smartphones spend comparatively less time with family than those who don't. A curfew on smartphone use after 9pm will help them to spend more quality time with their family.

The opponents think that imposing a curfew on young people's smartphone use is unfair. First, teenagers use smartphone for various educational and social purposes. Inflicting a curfew may keep students from searching for the information they need for their homework. After long school hours, evening is the only time for them to do their homework and other school related activities. Second, imposing a curfew on teenagers for smartphone usage is depriving them from their rights to use their smartphones. Teenagers are an important part of the society. Imposing unnecessary curfews on them may hurt their feelings and this might keep them from gaining confidence and becoming responsible members of society.

In conclusion, it is very important to create a balance between the use of smartphones and spending time with family. Smartphones are great tools for students for browsing the internet for new information and getting connected with their peers. However, moderate use of smartphones can enhance their benefits with mitigated damage to family relationships. It is the duty of the media to educate people of all ages in the proper use of smartphones to maximize their benefits with minimal side effects.

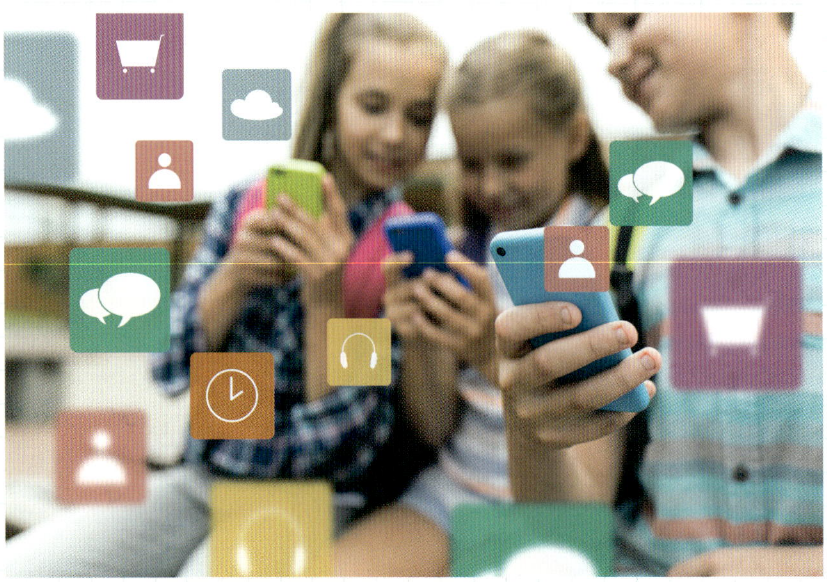

Main Exercises

1 Answer the questions.

Q1. How can a curfew provide benefits to a teenager?

Q2. According to the report, what effects do smartphones have on people?

Q3. What are the negative effects of a smartphone curfew?

Q4. Why are smartphones considered good tools for students?

Q5. How much time does an average Korean teenager spend using smartphone?

2 Fill up the blanks using the words below.

curfew *maximize* *distraction* *browsing* *imposing*

1. Most university students have………………… set by their parents.
2. Smartphones can be a ………………… when studying.
3. The average teen spends two hours …………………… the internet.
4. By turning off smartphones when working, we can ………………… working efficiency.
5. ……………… a curfew on teenager might make them even more rebellious.

3 Match the phrases to those given below.

1. Every technology is good when in moderate use.
2. It is important to maintain a healthy family relationship.
3. To create a balance between smartphones and spending time with others may be hard.
4. In most advanced countries

a. But it will definitely be worth the effort.
b. Try turning off your phone and chat with your parents.
c. Most people suffer from wrist arthritis from smartphone addiction.
d. Problems occur when they are abused or overused.

4 Summary

Fill the blanks up using the words given below and complete the summary.

average, entertainment, aid , curfew, prevent, imposing, unfair

Smartphones are one of the greatest inventions of modern age. Korea has the highest rate of smartphone users, and the ________ Korean teenager spends two hours every day using his smartphone. However, some believe that a ________ for smartphones after 9pm is necessary. They think ________ a curfew will _______students in their studying and spend more time with family members. The opposition believes that a curfew is________, because teenagers use smartphones not only for__________, but for educational or social purposes as well. Also, a curfew might hurt their feelings and this might ________ them from becoming responsible members of society. It is crucial to find the balance between family time and smartphone time.

5 Find the mistake in each sentence and correct the underlined words.

1. Smartphone usage may distraction students from studying.
2. Students can learn a lot through browse through the Internet.
3. Study efficiency can be maximize through many means such as setting a timer, removing disturbance, and keeping a progress journal.
4. Impose unfair rules on children may yield adverse effects.

6 Discussion Questions

Q1. How much time do you spend using your smartphone? Do you think it is too much or too little?

Q2. Why do parents set a curfew on teenagers?

Q3. Does a smartphone really serve as a distraction for all students who study? Why or why not?

Q4. What kind of activities can teenagers do with their family?

7 Writing Time

Is imposing a curfew on student's smartphone use helpful? Will it be a cure for smartphone addiction or will it cause problems for the child? Provide reasons and examples to support your answer.

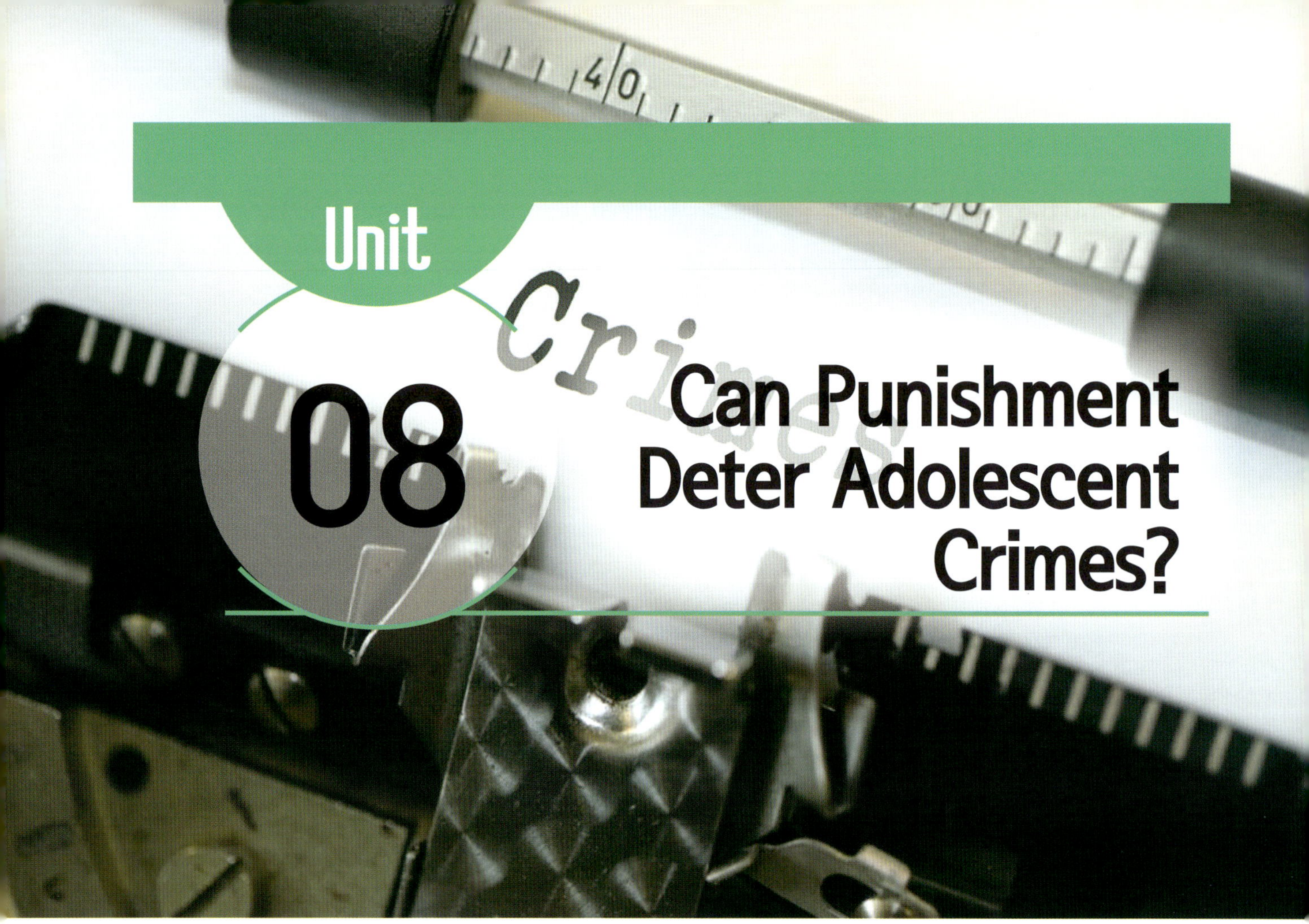

Unit 08 Can Punishment Deter Adolescent Crimes?

Warm Up Exercises

01 **Answer these questions.**

1. What kinds of people are criminals?
2. Name at least 3 kinds of crimes.
3. How old is an adolescent?

02 **Put the words in right column.**

Arson, Stealing, Execution, Prison sentence, Social service, Murder

Crime	Punishment

Pre-Vocabulary Exercises

1 Match the words to their similar meaning.

1. Discourage	**a.** Figures
2. Statistics	**b.** Penalty
3. Asset	**c.** Crime
4. Punishment	**d.** Strength
5. Juvenile	**e.** Young
6. Wrongdoing	**f.** To dampen one's spirits
7. Enforcement	**g.** Execution

2 Find the meaning of the following phrases.

1. Juvenile criminal ______________________________

2. Law enforcement ______________________________

3. Follow suit ______________________________

4. United Nations ______________________________

Can Punishment Deter Adolescent Crimes?

Youth is a priceless asset for any country that helps to shape a country's future. At the same time, more and more adolescent crimes are becoming concerns for law enforcement authorities in many countries. There is a lot of debate over how teenage criminals should be punished. In recent years, the rate of youth crime has increased sharply. United Nations statistics report that most young criminals are parts of big and organized criminal groups or they join disorganized street gangs. Due to the increase in crimes, many experts suggest increased punishment for juveniles. Is punishing adolescents a good way to control crimes?

People who think juveniles should be punished argue that every individual in society is responsible for their actions. First, a fear of punishment may keep many young people away from crimes. Most big gangs recruit young people because they know youths will not be prosecuted. However, suggesting punishment for criminals regardless of their age may discourage them from committing crimes. Second, laws should be implemented without any prejudice of age or gender. Giving an advantage of age to a criminal may encourage many others to follow suit.

Opponents of juvenile criminals' punishment argue that punishment has never been a great method of solving problems. First, punishment leads to more violent behavior. A teenager punished for a crime, may react more violently in the future. Second, some volunteer community service could be suggested for adolescent criminals instead of severe punishment. This may give them a chance to think about their wrongdoing and become better people. In addition, teenagers are immature in their judgments, therefore, a chance should be offered to them to make amends.

In conclusion, laws should be fair and transparent for all citizens in society without any discrimination. However, children who commit crimes for the first time must be given a chance to learn from their mistakes. It is the responsibility of the parents to keep a close eye on their children and on the company they keep. The government should open some counseling centers where children, who are tempted towards crimes, could get some advice and support.

Main Exercises

1 Answer the questions.

Q1. Why do big gangs recruit young people?

Q2. According to the UN statistics, what are most young criminals part of?

Q3. What benefits can social service give to young delinquents?

Q4. Whose responsibility is it to keep a close eye on children?

Q5. How should laws be implemented?

2 Fill up the blanks using the words below.

punishment *community* *juvenile* *enforcement* *statistics*

1. Lawbreakers will face severe ....

2. According to .... , there is a chance that criminals will commit the same crime again.

3. It is a better idea to help .... delinquents to become a better person rather than locking them up in prisons.

4. Law .... officers have the right to use force if necessary.

5. Young criminals are a problem in this ....

3 Match the phrases to those given below

1. The united nations have reported that

2. Young people have the tendency to follow suit as their peers.

3. Most juvenile criminals are not sent to jail.

4. Law enforcement personnel have the right to use violence.

a. Most young criminals join large organized gangs or unstable street gangs.

b. Because they feel that they are part of an organization or a group.

c. If they are threatened.

d. Instead they are sent to social service or released with a warning.

4 Summary

Fill the blanks up using the words given below and complete the summary.

juvenile, punishment, wrongdoers, transparent, community, prosecuted, discourage

There is a lot of debate whether teenage criminals should be or not be punished. People who believe that these ______________ delinquents should be punished argue that everyone in society is responsible for their actions, and teens are no different. ______________ may ______________ young people from committing crimes, and most big gangs use young people for crimes because they know that they will not be______________. Also, law should be implemented without prejudice, and giving an advantage of age to a criminal may encourage others to follow suit. People who oppose punishing young ______________ state that punishment has never been a great method of solving problems. In addition, they say that volunteer ______________ service may be a better option than punishment as well. Law should be fair and ______________ for all, but children must be given a second chance to correct and learn from their mistakes.

5 Find the mistake in each sentence and correct the underlined words.

1. Yesterday, some law enforce officers were injured while attempting to capture a criminal.
2. It is wrong to not punishing people for their wrongdoings.
3. Punishing criminals may to discourage others from committing crimes.
4. Through education, juveniles may able be to lead a clean life rather than a life full of crime.

6 Discussion Questions

Q1. Do you think giving juvenile criminals a second chance will make them a better person?

Q2. What kind of crimes do young criminals commit?

Q3. How can we keep young people from committing crimes?

Q4. Should the law allow exceptions in certain cases?

Q5. How would you feel if someone you knew was a criminal?

7 Writing Time

Should young criminals be punished severely or not? Will it lower crime rates or not? State reasons and provide examples to support your opinion.

Unit 09 Does Deforestation Help Humanity?

Warm Up Exercises

01 **Answer these questions.**

1. What is deforestation?
2. Name at least 3 kinds of trees you know.
3. Name at least 2 kinds of recyclable trash.

02 **Put the words in right column.**

Tissue papers, Plastic, Bottle, Food, Slipper, Egg, Skin, Fruit pits, Juice cans

Recyclable	Trash

Pre-Vocabulary Exercises

1 Match the words to their similar meaning.

1. Deforestation	**a.** being too crowded
2. Overpopulation	**b.** wipe out
3. Extinction	**c.** where a certain species lives
4. Habitat	**d.** related to the environment
5. Environmental	**e.** prohibition
6. Restriction	**f.** importance
7. priority	**g.** in the city
8. urban	**h.** wiping out forests

2 Find the meaning of the following phrases

1. Human being ______________________

2. Animal extinction ______________________

3. Vital part ______________________

4. Growing population ______________________

Does Deforestation Help Humanity?

Forests cover 30 percent of the earth's land. Forests are the main source of wood for heating and construction purposes for humans. Worldwide, more than 1.6 billion people rely on forest products for all or part of their livelihoods. Deforestation means converting forests into land for agriculture and urban use. Deforestation is one of the major causes of environmental problems and animal extinction. It is estimated that up to 28,000 species are expected to become extinct in next 25 years due to deforestation. Poverty, overpopulation, and unequal land access are the main causes of man-made deforestation. Is deforestation really more helpful to human than the damage it is causing to mankind?

Some people argue that deforestation is more helpful than harmful to humans. First, a large number of people in the world depend on forest related products for their income as the main purpose of forest is to provide a nonstop supply of wood for human needs. Putting restrictions on this industry could cause many people starve. Second, following the growing population and human needs, deforestation is inevitable. Every child that is born adds the needs for forest related products. Therefore, some experts think that the priority should be given to human beings and their needs for survival.

On the other hand, opponents of deforestation argue that forests are a vital part of human life. Human life may not exist if the forests disappear. First, forests control the ecosystem on the planet. 20 percent of the world's oxygen is produced in the Amazon forest. We cut trees for our daily needs, but this actually decreases our chances of survival on the planet in the long term. Second, deforestation is the major cause of animals'extinction. With decreasing habitats, some animals are starving to death. Cutting too many trees is also causing an imbalance between living things and their habitats on the planet. Considering the usefulness of certain species, their extinction can cause epidemics which may prove fatal for human existence.

In conclusion, it is our responsibility as human beings to understand the dangers of deforestation for our planet and for our future generations. The government should educate people about the damages caused by deforestation for our planet. It is important to maintain a check and balance system on illegal logging. Planting trees in towns at least twice a year should be one of the basic responsibilities of every citizen. In addition, a culture of using recycled items should be promoted worldwide to control deforestation.

Main Exercises

1 Answer the questions.

Q1. How many people depend on products from forests for their livelihood?

Q2. What are the causes of man-made deforestation?

Q3. How much of the world's oxygen is produced in the Amazon forest?

Q4. What kind of problems do decreasing wildlife habitats cause?

Q5. How many species are expected to become extinct in the next 25 years?

2 Fill up the blanks using the words below.

priority *deforestation* *restrictions* *overpopulation* *extinct*

1. Technological advances have led to .... of the Earth.
2. Strict .... must be imposed to prevent forests from disappearing.
3. Many animals are losing their habitats from ....
4. It is the utmost .... for humanity to protect the Earth.
5. Dodos became .... because of insufficient evolution and overhunting.

3 Match the phrases to those given below.

1. Human beings are the only species.
2. Animal extinction is becoming a problem.
3. Technological advances have led to less deaths which has resulted in a growing population.
4. Recycling plays a vital part in preventing deforestation.

a. As more and more natural habitats are becoming polluted.

b. Because it leads to cutting down less trees to produce more items.

c. And now the Earth is overpopulated.

d. Which destroys its own habitat

4 Summary

Fill the blanks up using the words given below and complete the summary.

deforestation, take action, habitats, inevitable, vital part, agricultural, imbalances, responsibility

Forests cover about a third of the Earth's land, and it is used for many purposes. Deforestation means converting forests into land for _________ or urban use. Some people believe that ________ is helpful to humans than harmful because there is a non-stop demand for wood products. Not only that, but following the growing population and human needs, deforestation is _________. On the other hand, others say forests are a _________ of life, as forests control the ecosystem of the planet. The Amazon forest produces 20% of the world's oxygen. People cut down trees in the amazon, which could lead to decreasing our chances of survival. Plus, cutting down could cause __________ between living things and their ________. It is the __________ of humans to understand the dangers of deforestation for the planet and for our future generations. The government and people should ________ to prevent deforestation from happening.

5 Find the mistake in each sentence and correct the underlined words.

1. Overpopulation is <u>become</u> a major problem in cities.
2. If deforestation <u>keep</u> on happening, humans may face extinction in the future.
3. Recycling and planting trees are a vital part in <u>prevent</u> deforestation.
4. Many environmentalist groups <u>is</u> trying to advertise the dangers of deforestation.
5. Not only does the Amazon forest produce oxygen, but it also <u>serve</u> as a habitat for many species of plants and animals.

6 Discussion Questions

Q1. How can we prevent illegal logging?

Q2. How can we prevent deforestation?

Q3. What are the negative effects of unequal land access?

Q4. Will stopping deforestation prevent species from becoming extinct?

Q5. How can we use fewer wood-based products in our lives?

7 Writing Time

Is deforestation harmful for humans? Why or why not? What are the pros and cons of logging? State reasons and provide examples to support your opinion.

Unit 10 Is Online Banking Helpful?

Warm Up Exercises

01 **Answer these questions.**

1. What is online banking?
2. Have you ever used online banking?
3. Name at least 3 banks you know.

02 **Put the words in right column.**

Bank, Banker, Hospital, Doctor, Firefighter, Police station, Clerk

Buildings	People

Pre-Vocabulary Exercises

1 Match the words to their similar meaning.

1. Financial	**a.** trustworthy
2. Procedures	**b.** to take money out of a bank
3. Loans	**c.** doing business
4. Withdrawal	**d.** steps
5. Physical	**e.** mortgages
6. Transaction	**f.** actions related with using body strength
7. Reliable	**g.** related with money

2 Find the meaning of the following phrases.

1. Safety procedures ______________________________

2. Online banking ______________________________

3. Basic functions ______________________________

4. Financial matters ______________________________

Is Online Banking Helpful?

Banks are considered the most reliable financial institutions around the world. The basic function of banks is that they keep our money safe. However, in this digital age, when most financial activities take place through computers or smartphones, physical banks are losing their relevance. Online banking is getting more and more popular because it is convenient and faster. Do we still need banks nearby our houses, or can online banking be more helpful?

Some people think banks are more reliable and convenient resources for addressing our money related matters. Firstly, there are lots of basic functions that regular banks perform including money transactions, deposits, withdrawals, currency exchange, and applying for loans. All these functions are not easy to perform through online banking for many people. Secondly, dangers associated with online banking including hacking cause constant concern for common users. Sometimes hackers are able to steal money from online accounts. In addition, the safety procedures for online accounts have made online banking activities more difficult which causes hesitation for some people to fully go online for their banking related matters.

On the other hand, opponents of physical banks think that banks are unnecessary in this age of digital development. First, most people are too busy to go to banks for their daily financial matters. Online banking provides customers easy to operate websites to make transactions and different inquiries. Second, online banking is also faster than physical banks. People need to stand in line and wait for their turns before they can do their banking. In addition, online banking is available almost 24 hours a day, all year round. This helps users do their banking whenever they want.

In conclusion, banks are a reliable place where people can easily deal with their financial matters. And technology has taken banks one step further by providing the public with a facility to do their banking wherever and whenever they want. In order to address the issues of security and reliability of online banking, both the government and the banking industry should try to make it safer and more reliable to reduce the threats from hackers.

Main Exercises

1 Answer the questions.

Q1. Where do most financial activities take place in the digital age?

Q2. What problems do safety procedures for online accounts have?

Q3. When is online banking available?

Q4. How can hackers be a problem for online banking?

Q5. What kind of service does online banking provide?

2 Fill up the blanks using the words below.

physical *procedures* *loan* *reliable* *financial*

1. Most .... matters can be taken care of at the bank.
2. You need to take certain .... before opening a bank account.
3. Some people think .... banks are more reliable than online banks.
4. People sometimes ....money from banks to buy houses or cars.
5. With high-level security programs, online banks can be as ....as real banks.

3 Match the phrases to those given below.

1. Financial matters can be taken care of at the bank.
2. The modern age has enabled us to use online banking.
3. In order to use online banking, you must follow a few safety procedures.
4. One of the basic functions of banks

a. Is to keep the customer's money safe.

b. With the help of a banker.

c. Which is convenient in many ways.

d. So that your account is kept safe.

4 Summary

Fill the blanks up using the words given below and complete the summary.

handle, basic functions, convenient, reliable, financial matters, procedures, physical

Banks are one of the most _______ financial institutions worldwide, keeping our money safe. Recently, online banking is becoming a trend because it is _________ and faster. Some believe that banks are more reliable and convenient because they are better at performing ___________ compared to online banking. Also, hacking and the complicated safety _________ are a concern for some people as well. However, opponents of _________ banks support online banking because many people are too busy to visit banks to _______ daily __________. Not only that, online banking is available almost 24 hours a day, and it is much faster as well.

5 Find the mistake in each sentence and correct the underlined words.

1. Online banking has the danger of hackers steal money from them.
2. The basic function of banks is to keeping the client's money safe.
3. Some people still use physics banking because it is simple.
4. You needing to take certain steps to get a loan from the bank.

6 Discussion Questions

1. What are the negative effects of physical banks?
2. What will happen if all banks are turned into online banks?
3. Why do online safety procedures make banking complicated and difficult?
4. How can we make an online bank account?

7 Writing Time

Should we all use online banking system? Why or why not? What are the pros and cons for online banking? State reasons and provide examples to support your opinion.

Unit 11 Can Korea be More Multicultural?

Warm Up Exercises

01 Answer these questions.

1. What does multicultural mean?
2. What does monoculture mean?
3. Name at least 3 examples of culture.

02 Put the words in right column.

Kimchi, Baguette, Waffle, Samgyupsal, Hanbok, Croissant

Korean	European

Pre-Vocabulary Exercises

1 Match the words to their similar meaning.

1. imagination	**a.** having more than one culture
2. globalized	**b.** mostly
3. discrimination	**c.** having only one culture
4. ethnicity	**d.** diversity
5. monoculture	**e.** being treated unequally
6. mainly	**f.** known and used worldwide
7. multi-culture	**g.** thoughts in one's head

2 Find the meaning of the following phrases.

1. Multicultural society ______________________________

2. Globalized world ______________________________

3. Unique culture ______________________________

4. Refer to ______________________________

Can Korea be More Multicultural?

Culture means a group of people who share common values. Culture also means the community in which we are born that includes race, origin, gender, or social class. Culture can also refer to a community we become a part of. When people from different cultures live together that is called multicultural. Korea is mainly a monocultural society. However due to many foreigners'arrivals into Korea, it is becoming more and more a multicultural society. Is a multicultural Korea better than a monocultural Korea?

Some people think that multicultural Korea will enhance Korean image internationally. Firstly, having many expats living in Korea will change Koreans' views about the world. This will broaden people's imagination and will help them to learn about other cultures. In addition, sharing ideas with different people in a multicultural society will help Korea's social and economic development. Secondly, a multicultural Korea will attract talented people from all over the world. This will brand Korea as a global and multicultural country to live. The United States, Canada, and the United Kingdom are some of the greatest examples of multicultural societies.

Opponents of a multicultural Korea argue that this will not be helpful for Korean economy and society. First, a multicultural Korea may harm the Korean identity and its unique culture. Korean traditions are based on more than 5000 years of history. Having people from all different races and ideas may result in identity loss. Second, having people from many different ethnicities or ideas may cause violence among locals and immigrants. This can also promote racial discrimination. Racial discrimination incidents happen sometimes in multicultural countries like United

States or United Kingdom.

In conclusion, there are lots of benefits of being a multicultural society. However, it is important to maintain the basic values of each culture. In this globalized world, multicultural societies are successful because of mutual cooperation and understanding. In order to establish an ideal multicultural society, each member of society has a responsibility to respect others' beliefs and ideas without any prejudice.

Main Exercises

1 Answer the questions.

Q1. What are some examples of multicultural societies?

Q2. What are Korean traditions based on?

Q3. What kind of action should be taken in order to form an ideal multicultural society?

Q4. What is the definition of culture?

Q5. What kind of benefits can a multicultural Korea bring to its people?

2 Fill up the blanks using the words below.

globalized *mainly* *imagination* *multicultural* *ethnicity*

1. As the world gets more and more ...., we can learn more about other cultures.
2. .... is the key to creativity and success.
3. The army is consisted of .... men soldiers.
4. Monocultural societies are made up of one ....
5. More and more countries are becoming ....

3 Match the phrases to those given below.

1. A multicultural society will
2. It is unwise not to change in this globalized world.
3. Unique culture should be respected.
4. The U.S is often referred to as

a. People must learn to accept and understand differences.

b. Broaden people's imagination and help them learn about other cultures.

c. An example of multicultural society.

d. Or disputes can occur.

4 Summary

Fill the blanks up using the words given below and complete the summary.

broaden, multicultural, loss, monocultural, discrimination, ethnicities, prejudice

Culture is a group of people who share common values. A place where people from different cultures are living together is called a ________ society. Some people believe that a multicultural Korea will enhance Korea because it will __________ the imaginations of people, and help them learn about other cultures. Also, it will attract people from all over the world. However, some believe in a __________ Korea because it may hurt the economy and cause identity ___________. Also, having many different ___________may result in ___________ as well. In order to establish an ideal multicultural society, each member of society has a responsibility to respect others' beliefs and ideas without any ___________.

5 Find the mistake in each sentence and correct the underlined words.

1. Modern technology has made the world become <u>globalize</u>.
2. Multicultural societies tend to be more <u>diversity</u> compared to monocultural societies.
3. <u>Discriminate</u> may become a problem in multicultural societies.
4. It is important to <u>maintaining</u> the basic values of each culture.

6 Discussion Questions

1. Do you like multicultural societies? Why or why not?
2. Why do people of different cultures fight with each other?
3. How can cultural diversity harm a country's identity?
4. What are the benefits of monocultural societies?

7 Writing Time

Do you think multicultural society is a good idea? Is it helpful, or will it make the uniqueness of cultures disappear? What are the pros and cons of multi-culture? Provide reasons and examples to support your idea.

Unit 12 Is Eating Out Better Than Eating In?

Warm Up Exercises

01 **Answer these questions.**

1. What is eating out?
2. Name at least three places where you can eat out.
3. Name at least 3 kinds of cooking methods.

02 **Put the words in right column.**

Stir-fry, Salt, Pepper, Boil, Steam, Glaze, Vinegar, Garlic

Cooking methods	Ingredients

Pre-Vocabulary Exercises

1 Match the words to their similar meaning.

1. Booster	**a.** not healthy
2. Linked	**b.** something that increases the effect of something
3. Unhealthy	**c.** related to
4. Cooking	**d.** time table
5. Availability	**e.** personal interest
6. Schedule	**f.** accessibility
7. Hobby	**g.** culinary

2 Find the meaning of the following phrases.

1. Whole grains ______________________________

2. Booster chemical ______________________________

3. Eating out ______________________________

4. Life style ______________________________

Is Eating Out Better Than Eating In?

Food is one of the most important parts of our lives. People have different eating preferences based on their lifestyles. Studies show that the number of people cooking and eating at home is decreasing in America. People's busy work schedules and the vast availability of delicious food in almost every town could be the reason why people, nowadays, tend to eat at restaurants more than in the past. Some people stay always ready to challenge themselves and try new foods at different restaurants, whereas, others prefer to cook and eat the same set of food at home. Do you prefer to eat out or eat in?

People who think eating out is benign present two main reasons to support it. Firstly, eating out saves a lot of cooking time at home. Cooking keeps people from choosing hobbies and enjoying free time. Cooking is sometimes dangerous because it involves fire and knives. Eating out helps people try various delicious foods at different restaurants. Secondly, eating out helps to develop social skills. In most cases, meals at restaurants take longer than the ones people eat at home. That gives families opportunities to have longer conversations. Eating out shapes an ordinary restaurant meal into a nice family gathering.

On the other hand, opponents of eating out think it is unhealthy. Firstly, homemade food is generally considered more nutritious. People who cook at home eat fewer calories and more fiber, calcium, and iron. Homemade food seldom has harmful taste boosting chemicals like MSG. Increasing cooking at home has also been linked to more consumption of fruits, fresh vegetables, and whole grains. Secondly, eating out is more expensive than eating in. Most people end up paying heavy bills for their meals. With a similar amount of money,as for eating out, they can buy enough healthy food for the whole family. In addition, some people argue that eating in causes a waste of time that could be used more efficiently. However, eating out can take as much time when one includes the time needed to go to the restaurant, to wait, and time to come back home. Furthermore, some people enjoy cooking as a hobby that gives them feelings of pride when they serve food to their families and friends.

In conclusion, whey deciding whether to eat out or stay in and cook, it is important to consider the potential health benefits of each of them. Eating out, typically considered less nutritious than eating at home, is not necessarily unhealthy. Some food lovers consider eating out more delicious, more satisfying, and quicker. However, others think that eating at home is healthier, time saving, and more nutritious. Following individual life styles and requirements, it is important to make choices that are safe, satisfying, and beneficial. What would you prefer?

Main Exercises

1 Answer the questions.

Q1. How can cooking be dangerous sometimes?

Q2. What does home-cooked food contain less of than food served when eating out?

Q3. Why do most people enjoy cooking as a hobby?

Q4. Does eating out mean it is less healthy than eating at home?

Q5. Is the number of people eating at home increasing or reducing in America?

2 Fill up the blanks using the words below.

unhealthy *hobby* *schedule* *linked* *cooking*

1. Junk food is very ....
2. Home .... can save money we spend for eating out.
3. It is a nice idea to have a .... to make good use of spare time.
4. Eating healthy food is closely .... to healthy lifestyles.
5. It is better to have a well-planned .... than none at all.

3 Match the phrases to those given below.

1. Whole grain bread may taste bad.
2. MSG is an example of a booster chemical.
3. Eating out may be the best option.
4. Some people prefer a carefree lifestyle.

a. When going on a date with someone special.

b. Which is harmful to the body but enhances flavor.

c. But it has high nutritional value.

d. Whereas others prefer busy life.

4 Summary

Fill the blanks up using the words given below and complete the summary.

components, nutritious, advocates, decline, availability, potential

Food is one of the main __________ in our lives, yet people's busy work schedule and the vast __________ of delicious food is leading to the ________ of people eating at home. People who eat out claim that it saves a lot of time cooking at home, thus making space for hobbies or free time. Not only that, but cooking can be dangerous because it involves using fire and knives. Finally, eating out can aid in the development of social skills, as eating out serves as a nice opportunity to have longer conversations. However, _______ of eating at home claim that homemade food is __________ compared to restaurant food. Also, they claim that eating out can be a waste of money and time. Whether eating out or at home, the most important thing is to eat healthy and consider ________ health benefits.

5 Find the mistake in each sentence and correct the underlined words.

1. Homemade food is generally considered to be full of nutritious.
2. Food at restaurants often containing harmful chemicals such as MSG.
3. Studies show that the number of peoples cooking and eating at home is reducing.
4. cooking can be dangerous because it be involving using fire and knives.

6 Discussion Questions

1. How can restaurants use less MSG in their foods?
2. How can we take precautions when cooking at home?
3. Does eating out really help social skills?
4. What are some convenient tips when eating meals alone?

7 Writing Time

Is eating out a better solution in this busy era? Will it save time or add additional financial burden to consumers? What are the pros and cons of eating out? State reasons and provide examples to support your opinion.

Unit 13 Are Driverless Buses Reliable?

Warm Up Exercises

01 **Answer these questions.**

1. What is public transportation?
2. Name at least 3 kinds of public transportation.
3. How often do you ride a bus?

02 **Put the words in right column.**

Private car, Subway, Bike, Motorcycle, Skateboard, Ferry, Train

Public transportation	Private transportation

Pre-Vocabulary Exercises

1 Match the words to their similar meaning.

1. Congestion	**a.** Recognize
2. Negligence	**b.** Propose
3. Identify	**c.** Uncertain
4. Unreliable	**d.** Carelessness
5. Suggest	**e.** Crowded
6. Navigate	**f.** Suitable
7. Applicable	**g.** Direct

2 Find the meaning of the following phrases.

1. In light of ____________________

2. Latest technology ____________________

3. Saving revenue ____________________

4. Starting a campaign ____________________

Are Driverless Buses Reliable?

Public transportation is transport provided by the government to the general public that includes buses and trains. Public transportation offers mobility and freedom to people of all walks of life. It saves travel time, reduces traffic congestion, saves millions of gallons of fuel, and reduces carbon emissions. Despite their enormous benefits, increasing bus accidents caused by drivers'negligence have concerned the authorities. In most cases, long hours of driving have been identified as the main reason for such accidents in buses. In light of this growing problem, some experts suggest a complete change in the transportation system by introducing driverless busses in cities. This model has already been implemented in some countries, including Denmark and Germany. Even though the burden on drivers will be reduced, the critics who oppose this idea worry it could be unreliable and dangerous.

Proponents of driverless public transportation insist that due to the increased rate of accidents, driverless busses and other transportation offer a safer alternative. First, the buses can be controlled by a central computer system that is based on the latest technology. Multiple cameras, sensors, and GPS systems help buses and trains to navigate through the city without accidents. This helps passengers to enjoy safe rides to their destination. Secondly, the promotion of driverless buses will save transport companies a lot of revenue that could be spent to pay drivers. This revenue could also be used to bring more technologically advanced transport to the road.

Opponents of driverless public transportation argue that this idea is not yet applicable. Firstly, driverless transportation is still in the phase of experimentation and it will still need 30 more years to be perfected. In addition, despite the advanced technology, most people do not completely rely on technology and feel uncertain about it. Secondly, driverless public transportation will cause many drivers in this industry to lose their jobs. This big shift will cause unrest among those jobless people and their families. Furthermore, this could cause a big disruption in social infrastructure when the country is more technology dependent.

In conclusion, both arguments and counterarguments regarding driverless public transportation have their strengths. Even though, many people enjoy modern means of transportation, lots of other people are uneasy about driverless public transportation. It is important for the government to start a campaign for public consensus before any major change in society.

Main Exercises

1 Answer the questions.

Q1. What is the main reason for bus accidents?

Q2. Which countries have implemented driverless buses?

Q3. How are driverless buses controlled?

Q4. Why don't people rely on the technology?

Q5. What happens if many drivers lose their jobs?

2 Fill up the blanks using the words below.

congestion *suggest* *identify* *applicable* *negligence*

1. Seoul needs a new system to reduce traffic …………………..…. .

2. She was fired due to her ………...…………….. .

3. You need to …………………….. yourself at the gate.

4. My father ………………….. me to reduce playing games.

5. The new law is not ……………… .

3 Match the phrases to those given below.

1. Some experts suggest a new transportation system.

2. Driverless busses are safe.

3. Most people are not sure about driverless public transportation.

4. Driverless public transportation will cause a big disruption.

a. The system is operated by the latest technology.

b. Drivers' negligence is increasing bus accidents.

c. Many drivers will lose their jobs.

d. The technology is not yet perfect.

4 Summary

Fill the blanks up using the words given below and complete the summary.

government, increasing, consensus, negligence, experts, latest, disruption

Public transportation is transport provided by the ________________ to the public. However, ________________ bus accidents caused by the drivers'________________ is a big problem in spite of its many benefits. To resolve the problem, some ________________ suggest driverless public transportation. They argue that the new system is safe with its ________________ technology and it will save money. On the contrary, opponents believe that driverless public transportation system is not perfect. In addition, it will bring a social ________________ since a lot of drivers lose their job. In conclusion, the government needs to build public ________________ prior to a major change.

5 Find the mistake in each sentence and correct it by reshaping the underlined words.

1. Public transportation is transport provide by the government.
2. Bus accidents caused by the drivers' negligence is increase.
3. Driverless buses have implemented in some countries.
4. Most people do not completely rely technology.
5. Many people is uneasy about driverless public transportation.

6 Discussion Questions

1. What are the benefits of driverless public transportation?
2. Are driverless public buses really safe? Why or why not?
3. How long will it take for driverless buses to be common?
4. How can governments help drivers who lost their job due to driverless buses?
5. How can governments achieve a public consensus?

7 Writing Time

Why do we need driverless public transportation? Is it a gift for the public or a disaster? Are driverless buses necessary? Provide reasons and examples to support your opinion.

Unit 14 Do We Need Free Wi-Fi?

Warm Up Exercises

01 Answer these questions.

1. What is Wi-Fi?
2. Name at least 3 most common places where you can use Wi-Fi.
3. How many hours do you use the internet for per day?

02 Put the words in right column.

Accident, Autism, Free, Traffic jam, Shopping, Map, Addiction, SNS

Advantages	Disadvantages

Pre-Vocabulary Exercises

1 Match the words to their similar meaning.

1. Radio wave	**a.** having no wire
2. Wireless	**b.** continuous
3. Disrupt	**c.** turmoil
4. Up to date	**d.** disturb
5. Upheaval	**e.** electromagnetic wave
6. Promote	**f.** latest
7. In constant	**g.** popularize

2 Find the meaning of the following phrases.

1. Past decade ______________________________

2. Daily life ______________________________

3. Staying connected ______________________________

4. Causing accidents ______________________________

Do We Need Free Wi-Fi?

Wi-Fi is a technology that uses radio waves to help people connect with the internet. A Wi-Fi connection is established using wireless adapters to create a hotspot that provides users radio signals to be connected to the internet. Wi-Fi technology has been widely developed in the past decade. People can get connected to the internet almost anywhere; at home, at work, in libraries, schools, the airport, hotels, restaurants, and many other places. Considering the importance of Wi-Fi, the government has begun providing Wi-Fi at some public places including, parks, train stations, shopping malls, museums, etc. Despite the benefits of Wi-Fi access at public places, some people think it interrupts free movement in public places and disrupts daily life.

Proponents of Wi-Fi access at public places think it helps people to stay connected and up to date. Firstly, children can be in constant contact with their parents when they are out of their houses. This helps parents track where their children are and provides them with a feeling of security and relief. Secondly, having Wi-Fi access at public places saves a lot of time because people do not need to run back to their homes in order to connect to the internet if they need to get some quick information online. In addition, having Wi-Fi access in public places helps to find maps, discover new restaurants and shopping malls, and get in touch with their friends through SNS.

Opponents of Wi-Fi access in public places argue that it could cause disruption in daily life. Firstly, having free Wi-Fi access at public places could cause upheaval in traffic and other movement. It is often noticed that people who use the internet don't pay attention to their surroundings. If they are outside their houses, they mostly ignore the fact that it is their responsibility to be aware of their own and others' safety. This negligence often causes minor and sometimes major accidents. Secondly, people's reliance on digital devices will increase if Wi-Fi access is provided at public places. The society is already facing the side-effects of this addiction. In addition, increasing internet usage has been related to autism and other attitude related problems.

In conclusion, Wi-Fi is one of the most useful discoveries of the modern age. It has revolutionized most fields of human life that relate to the information access. However, its disadvantages are raising red flags on further development and its spread. It is important for both the government and the public to clearly analyze the benefits and drawbacks of Wi-Fi access before further promoting it.

Main Exercises

1 Answer the questions.

Q1. Which technology does Wi-Fi use?

Q2. Where can people use Wi-Fi?

Q3. Why do parents feel a sense of relief?

Q4. How can traffic accidents happen due to internet?

Q5. Which illnesses can excessive use of internet cause?

2 Fill up the blanks using the words below.

disrupt　　*up to date*　　*promote*　　*radio waves*　　*wireless*

1. MRI uses ....to create images of the body.
2. My headphone is .... so it is convenient.
3. Please do not .... me while I am working.
4. Keeping .... information is very important.
5. My job is to .... the company's new product.

3 Match the phrases to those given below.

1. Wi-Fi is one of the most useful inventions.
2. Wi-Fi makes parents feel relieved.
3. Wi-Fi saves a lot of time.
4. Wi-Fi could trigger traffic accidents.

a. They can be in contact with their children.

b. People do not need to go back to their homes for the internet.

c. Internet interrupts people's attentions to their surroundings.

d. People can get access to internet at almost anywhere.

4 Summary

Fill the blanks up using the words given below and complete the summary.

contact, analyze, daily, helpful, connect, public, related

Wi-Fi is a technology that helps people ______________ with the internet. Regarding the importance of Wi-Fi, the government has started producing Wi-Fi at ______________ places. Some people consider free Wi-Fi at public places very ______________ because they can keep in ______________ with their children with it. Additionally, people don't need to go back to their homes if Wi-Fi is available. However, others think free Wi-Fi could cause chaos in ______________ life. Internet is one of the reasons of accidents and attitude ______________ problems. To sum up, the government and the public must clearly ______________ pros and cons of free Wi-Fi before producing more.

5 Find the mistake in each sentence and correct it by reshaping the underlined words.

1. The society is already face the side-effects.
2. People can get connect to the internet.
3. It is notice that people who use internet are not careful.
4. Wi-Fi is one of the most useful discovery.
5. The disadvantages are raise red flags.

6 Discussion Questions

1. What are the attitude related problems caused by internet?
2. What are the side-effects of public Wi-Fi?
3. How does internet usage cause autism?
4. What are the advantages of public Wi-Fi?
5. Should government cut back on public Wi-Fi? Why or why not?

7 Writing Time

Do the advantages of public Wi-Fi outweigh the disadvantages? Should government make more public Wi-Fi or not? Provide reasons and examples to support your opinion.

Unit 15 Is Drinking a Problem in Korea?

Warm Up Exercises

01 Answer these questions.

1. What is alcohol?
2. Is drinking alcohol a good habit? Why or Why not?
3. Name at least 3 kinds of alcoholic beverages.

02 Put the words in right column.

Coke, Chicken, Popcorn, Beer, Rice, Rice wine, Fries, Stew

Beverage	Food

Pre-Vocabulary Exercises

1 Match the words to their similar meaning.

1. Excessive	**a.** too much
2. Mood	**b.** lack of water
3. Dehydration	**c.** atmosphere of a certain place/person
4. Consumption	**d.** ingesting
5. Alienation	**e.** unfriendliness
6. Beverage	**f.** drinks
7. Intoxication	**g.** meeting people
8. Socializing	**h.** being drunk

2 Find the meaning of the following phrases.

1. Ministry of health ______________________________

2. Consumed in excess ______________________________

3. Alcoholic beverage ______________________________

4. Work related stress ______________________________

Is Drinking a Problem in Korea?

Humans have always been looking for different forms of amusement. Alcohol is one of the most common sources of releasing work related stress and boosting mood. Alcohol is considered an integral constituent of parties and social events in many cultures across the world. In Korea, drinking alcohol is one of the most popular social activities. People drink alcoholic beverages for many reasons including expressing sadness, showing happiness, relieving stress, socializing, and discussing some issues. Sometimes people drink too much and cause law and order problems which worries some experts. Is drinking really a problem in Korea?

According to the statistics, Korea is one of the most alcohol consuming nations in the world. Some experts think consuming too much alcohol is a social problem. First, excessive alcohol consumption leads to various health problems. Short term effects of alcohol consumption are intoxication and dehydration. However, alcohol affects the brain and liver if consumed in excess. Second, excessive consumption of alcohol is associated with many social problems including domestic violence and law and order problems. In addition, consuming alcohol could be a big financial burden on people of modest means. The Korea's Ministry of Health and Welfare estimates the alcohol-related social cost in Korea is $20 billion every year.

On the other hand, proponents of drinking alcohol think that it is a part of Korean tradition. Firstly, drinking alcohol with friends and family strengthen bonds between them. Alcohol is considered a great source to encourage socialization that includes making new friends, getting closer, and becoming more friendly. Furthermore, drinking is also one of the social practices that keeps a person in a certain community. Avoiding drinking with certain people in a community may cause alienation. Secondly, alcohol is one of the best ways to reduce work related stress. Most people think that drinking alcohol is the only way to curtail work related worries. The fatigue of the whole work week could be released by enjoying drinks with family or friends.

In conclusion, alcohol could be severely harmful if consumed in excess. It not only damages a person's health, but also it causes disruptions in society. It is important to set our drinking limits which keep us within acceptable social norms. A campaign should be launched to persuade people to avoid excessive alcohol consumption. Media companies should also play their role by controlling alcoholic beverage advertisements. Celebrities may also contribute by not becoming a part of alcoholic beverage advertisements.

Main Exercises

1 Answer the questions.

Q1. How much is the alcohol-related social cost in Korea?

Q2. What negative effects can result from avoiding alcohol use?

Q3. What kind of problems may happen from alcohol consumption?

Q4. What is one of the most popular social activities in Korea?

Q5. How can celebrities help to overcome excessive alcohol consumption in society?

2 Fill up the blanks using the words below.

mood *alienate* *excessive* *intoxication* *beverages*

1. The .... is almost as important as the food during a date.
2. Alcoholic .... cannot be sold to minors under the age of 19.
3. The dangers of drinking include dehydration and ....
4. Members of a group may .... their peers for avoiding drinking.
5. A little alcoholic drink may be good for one's health, but not in .... amounts.

3 Match the phrases to those given below.

1. The ministry of health's decision to increase alcohol prices
2. Alcohol, when consumed in excess amounts
3. Loss of hair is one of the main symptoms of work related stress.
4. Mudslide is an alcoholic beverage.

a. Can cause serious health problems.

b. And it is a problem for middle-aged businessmen.

c. Which is easy to drink.

d. Have been met with much scorn.

4 Summary

Fill the blanks up using the words given below and complete the summary.

beverages, domestic, dehydration, community, alienation, mood, consuming, excess, norms

Humans have always been searching for different kinds of amusement, and alcohol is one of the most common source of releasing stress and boosting ________. In Korea, it is one of the most popular social activities. However, some worry that drinking too much is a problem because Korea is one of the most alcohol __________ nations in the world. Alcoholic ________ can lead to health problems such as intoxication and ________, and social problems such as law and order problems and ________ violence. On the other hand, advocates of alcohol claim that it is a great way to strengthen bonds between friends and family. Also, drinking is one of the social practices which keeps a person in a certain ________, and avoiding such occasions may cause ________. Alcohol can be severely harmful if taken in ________ , so we should set our drinking limits within social _______.

5 Find the mistake in each sentence and correct the underlined words.

1. Small talk can <u>creation</u> a pleasant drinking atmosphere.
2. Some beverages are best <u>serving</u> cold, while others are best served hot.
3. Quitting <u>to drink</u> can save a lot of money.
4. Avoiding drinking with people in a community or group may cause <u>alienate</u>.
5. Media companies should <u>advertisement</u> the dangers of drinking.

6 Discussion Questions

1. What are the benefits of not drinking alcohol?
2. How can we set our drinking limits?
3. Why do people feel a sense of belonging through drinking?
4. Why does consuming alcohol lead to violence?
5. What are some other ways to reduce stress?

7 Writing Time

Is drinking alcohol good for people? Why or why not? What are the pros and cons of drinking alcohol? State reasons and provide examples to support your opinion.

Unit 16 Are Solar Panels Effective?

Warm Up Exercises

01 Answer these questions.

1. What is energy?
2. What are solar panels?
3. Name at least 3 kinds of energies.

02 Put the words in right column.

Gas, Sunlight, Hydroelectric energy, Thermal energy, Wind, Coal, Oil

Eco-friendly energy	Fossil fuels

Pre-Vocabulary Exercises

1 Match the words to their similar meaning.

1. Install	**a.** to pass a hurdle of hardship
2. Essential	**b.** be able to buy
3. Domestic	**c.** household
4. Overcome	**d.** to place something so that it works
5. Related	**e.** well-being
6. Welfare	**f.** connected
7. Afford	**g.** necessary

2 Find the meaning of the following phrases.

1. Energy production ______________________

2. Domestic marketplace ______________________

3. Clear environment ______________________

4. Solar energy ______________________

Are Solar Panels Effective?

Energy is one of the most essential necessities for human survival. Most aspects of humans' daily life depend on energy. Hydroelectric energy, tidal energy, wave energy, and solar energy are some examples of the energy that we use today. Solar energy means capturing the heat of the sun and turning it into electricity for our home use. Solar panels convert the sun's light into usable solar energy. Solar panel technologies use the sun's energy and light to provide heat, light, hot water, electricity, and even cooling, for homes, businesses, and industries. In advanced countries, obtaining solar energy through installing solar panels is a growing trend in both the business and domestic marketplace. Does installing solar panels really meet people's energy needs?

Considering the benefits of solar energy, experts believe that we should install solar panels on each house. First, installing solar panels on each house could help overcome the energy crisis that many countries face. This could provide a steady electricity supply to each house. Once installed, the government does not need to spend as much money on electricity related projects and that money could be used for social welfare. Second, installing solar panels on each house will help countries' economies grow. It will boost the solar energy sector and will in turn create many jobs. It will also provide people free or very cheap electricity. Solar energy is a clean and harmless source of energy that can play a big role in facing environmental issues.

Opponents of installing solar panels think this is not a practically possible idea. First, the solar panel industry is not very developed and that means the cost of solar panels is too high for common people to afford. According to one estimate, it takes 5 years for a common panel installed at a house to pay for its price in terms of energy production and usage. Second, in some countries including Korea, it is mostly cloudy or foggy in winter. That means, no sun and no energy. In that case, people still have to buy electricity from the government. In addition, the current solar panels can store 20% of the energy they receive from the sun. That means average solar panels can convert only 20% of the energy into electricity and of the remaining 80% energy is wasted.

In conclusion, it is a great idea to include solar energy in our domestic use. The sun is an enormous source of energy which is harmless to our environment. This energy can reduce the use of fossil fuels, and therefore, our next generations may enjoy a life in a clean environment. However, the scientists and the government should work together to make solar panels more advanced, cheaper, and more energy efficient. It seems like the solar energy could be a great benefit to humanity.

Main Exercises

1 Answer the questions.

Q1. How much energy from the sun can a solar panel save?

Q2. How long does it take for a common household solar energy panel to pay for its price?

Q3. How does a solar panel make energy?

Q4. What are some kinds of energy we use today?

Q5. How can the next generation enjoy a cleaner environment?

2 Fill up the blanks using the words below.

installed	*domestic*	*afford*	*essential*	*overcome*

1. Solar panels are .... on rooftops of houses.
2. It will take time before solar panels are introduced to the .... marketplace.
3. Many people do not have enough money to .... solar panels.
4. Technological issues must be .... in order for solar panels to be more efficient.
5. It is .... to use eco-friendly energy to save the environment.

3 Match the phrases to those given below.

1. Power plants must increase energy production.
2. We must use public transport for a clean environment.
3. It will take some time before the solar panels are everywhere.
4. Solar energy is welcomed by businesses.

a. It is a growing trend.

b. To pass down to our future generation.

c. Or a blackout may occur.

d. Because it has lots of potential to grow.

4 Summary

Fill the blanks up using the words given below and complete the summary.

solar energy, economy, industry, panels, essential, possible, overcoming, domestic

Energy is one of the most ________ necessities in human survival, and recently, solar energy has become a trend. It uses solar panels to capture the heat of the sun and turn it into electricity. Experts claim we should install solar _________ on each house because it could aid in __________ energy crises which many countries face. Also, it will help the _________ to grow, because it will boost the solar energy sector and create many jobs. However, opponents claim that it is not a ________ idea, as the solar panel ________ is not very developed, meaning that the cost of the panels will be extremely expensive. Not only that, but in some countries, such as Korea, it isvery cloudy or foggy in winter, which make the panels obsolete. In addition, the current __________ panels can only convert 20% of the energy which it receives from the sun, and the rest is wasted. It is a wonderful idea to include solar energy in _______ use, but the government and scientists will have to work harder to make it cheaper, more efficient and advanced.

5 Find the mistake in each sentence and correct the underlined words.

1. Solar energy can reducing the use of fossil fuels.
2. Solar panel use sunlight to provide heat, light, and electricity.
3. Solar energy is a clean and harmful source of energy that can solve environmental issues.
4. Many experts stressing the need to install solar panels in every household.

6 Discussion Questions

1. What are the negative effects of fossil fuels?
2. How can we save the environment?
3. What kind of problems do other types of energy have?
4. What is the most efficient source of eco-friendly energy?

7 Writing Time

Should we keep nuclear power plants or shut them down? Is it a cheap, reliable source of energy, or will it kill us all? What are the pros and cons of nuclear energy? State reasons and provide examples to support your opinion.

| 저자약력 |

About the Author

Bilal Qureshi earned his Doctorate degree in TESOL at Queen's University Belfast, UK and currently teaches at Seokyeong University Seoul. He has been interested in variety of issues related to second language learners' motivation and skill development; and this series of books shows his dedication and passion toward this goal. Email: qureshi@skuniv.ac.kr

Acknowledgement

I want to thank everyone who helped me through this process especially the reviewer and proofreader Professor David Miller, whose hard work motivated me a lot. I also show my appreciation to Professor Uk Chang from Duksung Women's University, Zeeshan Qureshi, Kim Bora, Jeong MinGyu, Hwang Junsook, and above all, my mother whose constant encouragement helped me complete this project.

Progressive Debate Active 1

2019년 1월 20일 1판 1쇄 인쇄
2019년 1월 25일 1판 1쇄 발행

저 자 | BILAL QURESHI
발행인 | 이수영
발행처 | 도서출판 청람
서울시 마포구 독막로 288(대흥동, 세양상가 109호)
전 화 | 02)3272-2601~2
팩 스 | 02)3272-2603
이메일 | crbooks@daum.net
홈페이지 | http://www.crbooks.co.kr
등 록 | 2000.8.26. 제6-0509호

ISBN 978-89-5972-667-7 93740 [정가 13,000원]

Audio files:
www.crbooks.co.kr/progressiveActive1/